BALANCE
IS ORDER

BALANCE
IS ORDER

Living an Abundant Life

BIH Y. JOHNSON

XULON PRESS

Xulon Press
2301 Lucien Way #415
Maitland, FL 32751
407.339.4217
www.xulonpress.com

Unless otherwise indicated, Scripture quotations taken from the Holy Bible, New International Version (NIV). Copyright © 1973, 1978, 1984, 2011 by Biblica, Inc.™. Used by permission. All rights reserved.

Scripture quotations taken from the New King James Version (NKJV). Copyright © 1982 by Thomas Nelson, Inc. Used by permission. All rights reserved.

Printed in the United States of America.

Paperback ISBN-13: 978-1-66280-919-4
Ebook ISBN-13: 978-1-66280-920-0

TABLE OF CONTENTS

I thank God for giving me the grace to write these words. Thank you to my family and friends for encouraging me throughout the process. Special thanks to my loving husband Leroy Johnson, for his tremendous support for me to write this book.

This book is dedicated to my beautiful, loving and caring mother, Josephine Koukou, who taught me the skills of servanthood. Though she has gone home to be with the Lord, her memories of high level of service to all around her is ever present. I thank God for creating her and the time He allowed us to share with her.

INTRODUCTION

WE WERE DRIVING TO OUR OLDEST SON'S middle school soccer game one afternoon in the fall of 2017, when I heard an inner audible voice say, "Balance is Order." This lifted me up right away. I wanted to stay in the uplifting, so I pondered on the phrase indefinitely. I had been going through a personal transformation, and the words captured my mind. As I contemplated on the phrase, many thoughts came to mind: "that would make a great sermon," "I wonder what it means?" The more I reflected, the more I had a visual playback of my life from when I was a little girl in kindergarten up until that moment. One thing that stood out to me was the fact that I moved so many times. Nonetheless, it instantly felt like I was in the right place (my city), and I did not have to move locations again. With a smile on my face, I kept on driving, though I could not fully understand what the phrase was.

God was not only preparing me for my assignments, but He was also beginning a mending process in my new life.

The verse that would be later revealed for the phrase "Balance is Order," is

> **Romans 8:28**
> **And we know that in all things God works for the good of those who love him, who have been called according to his purpose.**

My prayer for anyone reading this book is that you find your balance no matter what stage of life you are in (teenager, young adult or seasoned adult) and that God reveals your purpose of existence to you.

There is an urgent need for everyone to be balanced especially if you want to live a happy and fulfilled life. When there is no balance in a person's life, it is difficult to stop and acknowledge blessings or achievements. We get so busy with our transactional lifestyles that we do not often stop to thank God for the things He has already done. In my case, I was usually overwhelmed by the fact that we had three children including a set of twins, although we had decided as a family that I stay home to take care of our children, some days felt like I was missing out on education, career, and social life. I was not paying attention to what

God was building or even thinking back on how imbalanced I felt even when I was still under my parents' care.

Though this book is written based on my own scenarios of how God transformed me from being imbalanced to being on God's orderly scale, it is a testimony to encourage anyone who wants to live the abundant life. Once your balance in God is attained, there will be order in your life and you will be able to experience an abundant life according to the promise spoken by Jesus Christ.

John 10:10
***The thief comes only to steal and kill and destroy;
I have come that they may have life and have
it to the full.***

As you read this book, my prayer once more is that you attain your Godly designed balance, first through the gift of salvation, then through the steps that God ordered for you when you were created. In this busy world we live in today, it is difficult to find balance in different area of our lives. Some of these area include, work, daily living, relationships (marriage, family, co-workers, friends and most of all, God), purpose, and raising children. The need for a balance begins at a young age. An unbalanced life can begin as early as middle school, through high school and continue as the transition to college and beyond is made. During this time, there is preparation and pressure to either go to college or go out and venture into the world putting to test everything learned from childhood. Parents are usually the balance until this time comes (starting from 18 years of age if you live in the Western world).

Proverbs 22:6
Train up a child in the way he should go, and when he is old, he will not depart from it.

The first taste of the world is between you and the deity you belong to (that is how you were raised and the Higher powers you believe in). If you are a Christian and have accepted the Lord Jesus Christ into your life, you are an heir to the Kingdom of Heaven. You are blessed because you have the Holy Spirit as your guide, which means He becomes your balance. In many cases, we want to experience life by ourselves without God's help as we think we have everything under control. This is when things can start spiraling out of control. They say hindsight is 20/20, as for me, if I knew in the past what I know now, I would never had made a single step without Christ.

When we first experience independence, it is typically when we are heading to college or to our first jobs (usually as a single person). Even though we only have ourselves to balance when beginning life as a young adult, there is still a need for balance. For instance, if you are in college, you need to balance schoolwork, college life, and different relationships. If you are working, you also need to do the same. We need this balance to successfully carry out day-to-day activities.

The more we advance in life, the more it becomes important for us to find balance in every step. Balance is defined as *an even distribution of weight enabling someone or something to remain upright and steady (Oxford Dictionary).* To be upright and steady, means there is stability, and no fluctuation in that person's life. (up today and down tomorrow).

For something to work perfectly, there needs to be order as well. Order is defined as *the arrangement or disposition of people or things in relation to each other according to a sequence, pattern, or method (Oxford Dictionary).* Order is needed in everything we do. If we do not have order, there will be chaos in our lives. Imagine a double beam scale when one end of it bears more weight than the other, it becomes imbalanced. To make it even, there is an up and down movement between both sides (chaos) until the sides are even. When it reaches the even state, there is some sort of stillness.

Chapter One:

WHEN IS BALANCE NEEDED?

IN MOST CASES, BALANCE SHOULD BE AN expected end when one embarks on a journey. That way, when you get to the end of the journey or season, there is a sense of fulfillment and stability. For instance, in the book of Genesis, we see that God created the earth and there was no form to it. He decided to put a form to beautify it with land, sea, and beautiful plants.

Genesis 1:1-2
In the beginning, God created the heavens and the earth. ² The earth was without form and void, and

dakness was over the face of the deep. And the Spirit of God was hovering over the face of the waters.

Now let us backtrack a little. God created the Heavens and the earth. Lucifer who is also known as Satan, was one of the angels, but his pride took over him, and God casted him out of heaven to earth and a third of the angels followed him. I believe part of the reason why God did not destroy Satan is because He wants everything to have a balance and order. He already knew that He would later create men and He wanted us to have "freewill" just like the angels who decided to follow Satan. Satan was out of order when he thought of himself as God's equal and wanted to share God's Glory. After he was casted out of heaven *(Luke 10:18 He replied, "I saw Satan fall like lightning from heaven")* to earth, there was a separation of good (God) and evil (Satan), hence establishing the first balance between heaven and earth. God could have eradicated Satan and decide to never create anything that would go against Him. He could have decided to destroy anything that was His opposite, but since He is a just God, a balance was instilled instead. When God reformed the earth, He only took seven days and intentionally made sure that there was an opposite to everything, to create a balance. Some examples of the opposites are light/darkness, man/

woman, water/land, creature of the sea/land, day/night, hot/cold etc. As we can clearly see, balance was and still is important to God, from creation until now, God has marvelously, consistently, shown it to us. To link this up to our day-to-day human life, before the creation of a new life happens, a male and female are needed for the process to take place. That is the genesis of our existence and it spreads out to different aspects of our lives. As we grow, we change stages either by taking on more at a time or less. There is a need to continually gauge our lives to know if we are balanced in our current season.

It is typical for this feeling to begin right around high school, as independence starts kicking in during this time. Parents often no longer assist with schoolwork (they cannot remember most of it). Children learn to manage their schoolwork, extracurricular activities, friends, and family. Next is off to college, where independence is heightened, and we start getting the taste of the real world. Many of the decisions that are made at this time usually follow us for the rest of our lives. If we get an education, it tailors our future. If we take more student loans than we need, it may hurt our finances in the future. We could also find the right partner to build our future with and start a family. Whatever we do, we still need to juggle and balance it all to keep order.

The fun part is when a career kicks in and we start building a family. With all these changes, there can be a lack of balance at each point, we begin to feel either stressed and overwhelmed or as if something is missing. This is when we often find ourselves in a quest for balance. There are always signs from the Creator (God) to bring the imbalance to our attention. However, we often miss the hints until changes occurs or something drastic happens.

The best approach when we feel imbalance is to pause and do the following:

Take inventory of your current state:

- Identify the thing that worries you the most and what you are about to do.
- Are you buying a home?
- Are you starting a new job?
- Are you in need of a car?
- Are you getting married?
- Are you going through a divorce?
- Are you mourning?
- Are your children doing well?
- Is your health under attack?
- Are you in school?

- Are your finances where they need to be?
- Are you longing to live a purpose driven life?

All these events are life changing and can offset your balance. Someone who is not balanced will not have total peace in these instances. It will be difficult for anyone to freely enjoy the blessings in their lives if their balance is off. When we consciously or subconsciously add responsibilities to our current season, or free ourselves from things we are used to doing, it determines the level of our balance. The duration of the imbalance is the length of time we spend adding or reducing things on our scale to get things to a stable or orderly state. If a family has grown children and those children do not think it is necessary for them to take care of their own responsibilities (believe it or not, it is very common), the parents often continue taking care of their children's livelihood (sometimes sacrificing their own balance). As a responsible adult, if we have too much going on without the necessary balance, we must sacrifice some of the things that we think we need to liberate space for the current season. We need to be able to enjoy and appreciate the current blessings we have. That is why in *Matthew 6*, after Jesus taught His disciples how to pray, He emphasized for them not to worry about what they will eat or drink. If God can take care of the birds in the air, how much more will He take care of us who are made in His image?

Matthew 6:34
Therefore, do not worry about tomorrow, for tomorrow will worry about itself. Each day has enough trouble of its own.

Ultimately, God is the only source of balance in our lives, and we cannot attain orderly balance if He is absent from our lives.

Chapter Two:

MY JOURNEY TO BALANCE: CHILDHOOD

I WAS BORN A SECOND CHILD OUT OF four children in a city called Bamenda, in the North West Region of Cameroon, West Africa. At that time, my parents were renting an apartment as my father's only property was in the village (what is referred to in the USA as "country") and his job was in the city. We lived there until I was about three years of age, then we relocated to a neighborhood called "Mile 3, Nkwen" (still in the same city) where my father built his second home. We lived there for about ten years; this is where I spent most of my childhood. I can remember that we had some good and some not so good times, just like any family. At a young age, I always felt like I was missing something, but since I could not explain it, I internalized and ignored it. My coping mechanism was to never take anything serious about life, it was easier to joke about everything. I was always known as the jovial child who was always happy and made everyone around her laugh (court jester). Though I would laugh and joke about everything, I still had that feeling of "missing something" deep inside.

My parents and four other families were the main members at a Baptist church (Menda Baptist Church, Nkwen) in the area, so we spent most of our time at the church cleaning, at children's choir practice, and with any other group practicing or cleaning. Besides the church activities, there was schooling, and that is where everything was serious. The problem was, I could not escape my reality by cracking jokes and being funny all day in school. Usually being that "court jester" in class got me in trouble. School became where I felt the most imbalanced because I got in trouble for playing in class or orchestrating the teams of play during class in preparation for the lunch break games. Of course, my performances were mostly average and my dad, as a Headmaster (Principal), would always tell me "no child that I have given birth to is not intelligent," that always put a smile on my face because he believed in me.

From my mother's perspective, she did not put any pressure on me about my performances, probably because she loved the fact that we were all different. She had once told my elder sister that she enjoyed our differences and that is why she treated us as individuals, even our punishments were different. The same approach did not apply to all. My average performance continued, and one dear neighbor "Pa Cook" gave me a French nickname "Madame Soixante et Un" meaning "Madam Sixty-One" which was my class position for promotion. Another name he called me was "promoted on trial." I laughed at the names but deep down inside I knew I could do better, but I did not know how to come out of the imbalance feeling.

When I began the sixth grade, I got in trouble with another student, and he promised he was going to "get me" after school. I knew that it was not going to be funny so right after school ended, I took off running home. My school was on a hill, I ran so fast I dropped my backpack while running down the slope and I could not go back to get it. When I got home, I did not want to tell my parents what happened, so I decided to put all my efforts into studying hard with my best friend, who was always one of the top three in class. By the end of that term, I went from the 61st to the 3rd position. That was the first time I got serious about anything in my childhood, and it proved to me that I could do anything if I got serious about it. There was now hope that I could get a "balanced" feeling in the future.

During that school break, my parents celebrated my success all summer long. I wanted to keep the feeling of being somewhat balanced and I did. While that season started with me feeling balanced, my parents started having a lot of problems in their marriage and that sense of imbalance presented itself once more. A couple of years later, my mom was getting her education in a Professional Teacher's School, and as part of her course, she had to go to another city which was about eight hours away for a year. I was about 12 years old and could comprehend that my father was not happy about my mother going that far to school. The country was going through an economic crisis and he told us that he had gotten about a seventy percent salary pay cut. My sister and I attended private boarding schools and the tuition became difficult to pay. My sister was in her final year and since my father could not afford to pay both of our tuitions, I had to stay at home for an entire term. Thinking about it, this caused a heavy deficiency in my balance, and I could feel my mental scale continuously fluctuating still without a balance.

My mom returned from school and after a brief discussion with my father, she enrolled us in schools nearby to her school as she still had two more years to finish. I was able to bounce back at school and this time I exceled, maybe because I felt like I missed an entire term. Eventually, my parents separated, and we never returned to our home in "Mile 3 Nkwen."

We moved to the economic capital (Douala) of Cameroon, where some sort of balance was established as my mom worked and owned a business. Unfortunately, she died after a couple of years, just a few days after my eighteenth birthday. This brought another level of not only imbalance but also confusion, uncertainty, hopelessness, despair, pain, anguish, and other raw emotions I had in me. As I look back, the blessing here was that a year prior to my mom's passing, her good friend had traveled to the United Kingdom and she advised my mom not to send my elder sister to the University in Cameroon. "Send her abroad where she can work, go to school, and secure a better future for herself," she said. My sister, who was only nineteen years old, living in Germany at the time of mom's passing, became our saving grace. God used her mightily at that young age to take care of her three younger siblings (maintaining our great education) and the rest of the family. There was still a hole in my heart, a void that no one could ever understand or fill but I knew God could deliver me. Anyone who has lost someone dear (be it through death, divorce, separation etc.) can relate to this type of feeling.

Chapter Three:

MY JOURNEY TO BALANCE: ADULTHOOD

I STARTED DRAWING BACK TO GOD, AS I had strayed away for a while. I realized that when my thoughts were in Him, it was the only time I felt peace. By the grace of God, my sister made a way for me to travel and join her in Germany when I was twenty. Together we tried the best we could to stay sane, attempting to fill and maintain the peace, joy, happiness, and protection that felt suctioned out when we lost our dear mother. She was a pillar to us, her children, her siblings and her widowed mother as well. After my relocation to Germany, I gained some independence, which gave me a boost and hope in life. Together, we traveled an amazing journey (all led by God) and became each other's support system. Our only source of strength was and will always be God. About a couple of months after I got to Germany; I ran into this very calm gentleman, it instantly felt like that stillness in the storm when Jesus spoke to it in Mark 4:39 when he said, "…Peace, be still!" He became a good friend and confidant of mine. I could be silly, serious, playful, or funny, and all he did was encourage me to be more myself. If I wanted to go out somewhere, he would not only take me, but he would ask me to invite my friends. In a very strange way, I felt safe around him. He became my best friend (still is) and has been my husband now for almost twenty years. Our relationship reminds me of how the apostles were sent in twos *(Mark 6:7 Calling the Twelve to him, he began to send them out two by two and gave them authority over impure spirits).* To me, it is an evidence of one of God's great promises that we arc never alone, He is always with us.

Though things were starting to look good for me as I progressed, I still did not feel the balance I desired. Shortly after I met my husband, he was deployed to "Operation Iraqi Freedom" in 2003 and there I was again, thinking to myself, there goes the stillness and progression to my balance. However, God did not let him go for a long period of time. He was only gone for three months, but not too long after he returned, I had admissions to further my studies at the University of North Dakota (UND), Grandforks, ND USA. Before I left Germany, we got engaged, and once again, I had to change places, and be separated from my support system (my sister and now fiancée). I lived with my cousin in Grandforks for about eight months while attending school.

After the spring semester, my then fiancée was sent back to Ft. Eustis, Virginia from Germany. I was looking forward to the feeling of stillness he provided to me as a companion (I always felt like with him I was on the right track of my balance journey). We got married in December of 2004, soon after we got married, he was sent on another deployment for a year in Afghanistan. The time he spent with me before deploying was only four months. This time things were a little different because we were newly married, and I was pregnant. My imbalance census was off the charts once more (new city, new life, new season, pregnant). Thankfully, my husband had been stationed in Ft. Eustis before, so as soon as we got there, we had a church home. I had a place I could go and cry out to the Lord for strength and sanity to maintain my peace, especially during the pregnancy. I felt my mom's passing even more during that season, and it did not help that I lived in this new place with no family members. I had to cling to God once more to sustain me. Our first son was born while my husband was still gone, but he was able to come for the delivery. When he finally returned from Afghanistan, he decided to retire from the military so we could concentrate on building our family. By this time, we had not lived in the same country beyond six months since we got engaged. We decided to move back to Georgia, where my husband is originally from and it has been the place where I have lived longest.

We continued to grow our family in Georgia, and God blessed us with a set of boy and girl twins. Through the twins, God provided a great support system to us by way of family, friends, and amazing neighbors. After the twins birth it was not feasible for me to work, I was able to stay at home. However, the feeling of imbalance did not go away. I enrolled in a two-year Associate's degree program in Accounting, completed the program, and got a job as an HR Specialist. This made things worse, in the sense that I was trying hard to fill my void with earthly things and I quickly got overwhelmed, still lacking the satisfaction I thought I would have. I had to quit the job after a couple of years because it was no longer possible for me to maintain as an employee, wife, and mother of small children, especially with the schedule I had. Something had to give and the first thing I sacrificed was my job as my family to me was non-negotiable. The moment I resigned, I felt empty and lost as I had spent more time at work than anywhere else. I shared these things with one of my sister/mentor Catherine Ngoh and she invited me to join her women's Bible study (Bible Studies Fellowship), which was more like a support group. I did not know what to expect from the studies, but it felt right in my heart; I knew it would take some worries away and fill some of the void I felt. Though the gesture from my mentor may have seemed very minimal, I believe it was a pivotal point in my life and the opening to the doorway of my calling. This time, the revelations I got from the studies were clear, I was in a good place to receive, and I started feeling some sense of balance and order in my life.

When we moved to Georgia, my husband took us to a local church, recommended by his friend. Though we attended my husband's home church Pleasant Grove Baptist Church in Rayle, GA, I later joined the local church we attended. Through consistent prayers, fasting, and guidance from those who God placed in my path, I heard my calling as an Evangelist and answered it. While serving in and out of the church, I had to be in training just like any process God takes us through, He prepares us for what is ahead. I got even closer to God because I knew that it was a privilege to be chosen as His vessel.

The faithful day I internally heard God's audible voice "*Balance is Order*" and was reminded by Him that the feeling of imbalance was always there because I could not settle anywhere else other than where I was. God revealed that He was the only one that could be the balance in my life and bring order to it. I used the title of this book as my initial sermon, little did I know it will morph into this. One of my wise Ministry Team Leads/Mentor, Min. Elliott Butler advised that the sermon was very condensed, and I needed to "break it down." I should have realized that there was more to the write up. All along, I did not know my whole existence, God had intended for me to find my balance in Georgia. This sums up my journey to a balanced life, and it is a continues process as things are changing according to God's will.

Relating this to the word of God, scripture reminds us that there is a plan for all of us.

Jeremiah 29:11
For I know the plans I have for you," declares the Lord, "plans to prosper you and not to harm you, plans to give you hope and a future.

If God can number the hairs on our heads *(Luke 12:7 and Matthew 10:30)*, He has a perfect plan for us. The challenge is, when we are in the flesh, we believe that we have control over our lives. However, the plan/purpose will not be revealed to us until the perfect time, when we can handle it. Had God revealed my purpose sooner than He did, I do not believe I would have seen Him the way I have in my recent years. Your purpose can easily be delayed or sabotaged if there is no balance. Without balance, it may be difficult to take an account of how things are going, recognize where you are doing too much or less, and appreciating your own efforts. When personal life changes present itself, there is a need for an adjustment and a new order. There are many examples in the Bible that show us how important balance is to God. Through these examples, we can learn to submit our lives to God and allow Him to bring the necessary balance in our lives.

Chapter Four:

BIBLICAL EXAMPLES OF BALANCE

Adam & Eve

ON THE SIXTH DAY OF CREATION, GOD created man (Adam) and gave him dominion over all His creation. He also knew Adam needed a companion, so He created Eve from Adam's rib.

> ***Genesis 2:18***
> *"The Lord God said, "It is not good for the man to be alone. I will make a helper suitable for him."*

Reviewing this aspect, this was the first marriage on earth, an indication that the two individuals become one; hence it is the model of all marital relationships. God could have molded another being to become a woman, but He intended for the couple to be together as one. During creation man was created whole with all body parts included (head, hands, feet, legs, heart etc.). Then God put him to sleep, removed his rib and created a woman (Eve) *Gen. 2:21*.

I believe that is why women seem to have it all together most often, because they are made of a "whole" rib from a body which is the missing rib from a man. I once was ministering to a couple of young ladies, they asked me a question "how do you get ready for marriage?" My response to them was, in order to be ready for marriage as a woman, you can start by thinking and visualizing yourself as married. Mentally design the life you anticipate living as a married couple. Ask yourself some of these questions; "where do I want to live?" "How many children would be ideal for me?" "What role can I play in a marriage?" Some of these questions will bring self-awareness and I believe that those thoughts are mostly brought to light by the Holy Spirit, especially if you are believer. I also advised them to make it a habit to call and check up on someone, have a welcoming attitude, start thinking of your own family traditions etc. The reason for this approach I used to answer these ladies' question (which can also be applied by man) was to encourage them to be whole and secure about themselves.

Most often, we get into relationships thinking it will make us whole where we are lacking (I initially thought so and I was very wrong). Only God can make us whole and that is only if we let Him. Though Eve was created from Adam's rib, God intended for her to be a whole human being, a companion, a helpmate, but not less than Adam. I always wondered why there are more single moms than single dads, or the phrase "independent woman" is more common than "independent man", but I came to realize that women function as a whole unit (you cannot miss what you never had, and a man is still lacking a rib until he finds it). Women may operate better than men in some independent respects, to be complete, there is a need to plug in to a body (getting married) according to the will of God for humankind, as both roles are very vital in the balance. By nature, a woman nurtures (both male and female) beginning from pregnancy, to childbirth, to the development of the child. On the other hand, God did not create a man to carry a baby in his body or naturally nurture, man was made to work and tend to His creation *(Gen. 2:15 The Lord God took the man and put him in the*

Garden of Eden to work it and take care of it). For a balance to happen in a reproductive marriage, both parties are equally needed. If both parties understand their roles, the balance will be attained faster, and we need God to grant the needed understanding. I believe God wanted to instill order, and at the same time symbolize the oneness in the body (ultimately the Body of Christ, which is the Church). God in all His wisdom created man and woman to depend on each other, so that we can have a perfect balance.

Prov. 18:22
"He who finds a wife finds what is good and receives favor from the Lord."

Think about it in a logical sense, if the first woman was made from a man's rib and the Bible says a wife is a "good thing" that can also mean a "good rib." This means that only God can bring you together with the right spouse who fits you. There must be a perfect fit for a man's missing rib, else there will be issues with the fitting. Now if the rib (wife) is too big (more mature) than the man, it will be off balance, maybe uncomfortable and an adjustment will be needed. If it is too small (not mature enough), then the man is still missing a rib because he still has a void. In this case, the couple will often have a lack of understanding in their relationship because they are not equally yoked. This can manifest as the man feeling like he is not enough, or he feels like he is still lacking and vice versa and some of these cases can end up in divorce. There may be some who are faced with a similar misfit situation; however, God is very intentional with the paths He places us on. Be encouraged as it could just be that the rib (wife) was plugged in to the body (husband) too soon and is still growing into the size or the body/husband is still growing to make room for the wife/rib to fit. If you are in this situation and desire to get better, the best approach is to be sure that you belong to God. Surrender to Him, make Him the center of your situation, and He will rescue you. If the union was ordered by God, it may just be a matter of time and patience for both parties to grow into the full will of God. The perfect fit will not hurt and will fill the void, there will be understanding in the marriage and ultimately a great balance.

A man functioning as a woman or vice versa is out of God's order, but God can turn any situation to His Glory (His thoughts are not our thoughts). Naturally, if a man and a woman do not come together, there will be no reproduction fulfilling God's will for mankind to increase in numbers and multiply *(Gen. 9:7)*. Therefore, there is an emphasis to marry the right person and only God knows who He created to fit whom. God gave us the freewill to choose what we want to do with our lives, either to be heirs of His Kingdom or not, either to partake in His will for mankind or not. That is one of the beauties about God, and all the choices have consequences, be it good or bad. For those who are not yet ready for marriage or do not have the desire, God maybe preserving you for another purpose. We all belong in His "Master Plan"

Joseph's Rejection was for Balance

God tremendously demonstrates balance in the life of Joseph. Joseph was the first son of Rachel, one of the two wives of Jacob. Rachel was the one Jacob loved and wanted to marry. Laban, Rachel's father who was also Jacob's uncle, had asked Jacob to work for seven years to win his daughter. Jacob did so, nevertheless Laban tricked him into marrying Rachel's elder sister (Leah) instead, because she was not yet married. Laban gave another condition to Jacob that if he still wanted to marry Rachel, he had to work for seven more years and Jacob did. Maybe God blessed Leah with children first because she was not loved by her husband, yet Rachel was childless for a long time.

Rachel had her servant Bilhah bore two sons with Jacob on her behalf, God finally heard her cry, and she became pregnant with Jacob's eleventh son. She named him Joseph, meaning "God has taken away my disgrace." The first sense of balance here is between Leah and Rachel. Leah was deemed to be more blessed when it came to childbearing. However, God kept Rachel from having children right away because Joseph was the one God used to rescue Jacob's entire family during famine and establish them in Egypt. One of the reasons why it is best not to envy someone else's blessings is because, as God's children, we are all blessed in one way or the other.

Though Joseph was favored by God, his path was not easy. His brothers were very jealous of how Jacob loved him and for that reason, they did not like Joseph. It did not ease the jealousy when Joseph had dreams about everyone in the family bowing down to him. Even his father was upset about the fact that he would bow down to his son Joseph. The favoritism from Jacob and Joseph's prophetic dreams steered the brothers to dump him in a pit and sell him to Egyptians. That act of wickedness led to Joseph going to Egypt as a slave. Eventually, he not only became second to Pharaoh, but through him, his family was favored during a severe famine and Joseph integrated his brothers to Egypt with Pharaoh's approval.

All his brothers were made leaders in Egypt and the 12 sons of Jacob became the 12 tribes of Israel. These things could not have happened if Joseph was not maltreated and sold to strangers. There is a balance between Joseph's trials and his reign. He needed one to complete the other. Through Joseph's process, God was positioning him to become a governor in a foreign land, where the Israelites would gather, increase in numbers, and become powerful in the land.

God restored the order He intended, as Joseph who was the first son of the woman Jacob loved, He honored the union by using Joseph as the saving grace for the whole family. Rightfully, it was Joseph's position to be the heir of Jacob's blessings from his father Isaac, but God chose Leah's son (Judah) instead (God is a just and fair God). Even though he was rejected by his brothers, Joseph ended up in a position that only God could have crafted, directed and justly balanced the entire family. (Joseph's story can be found in *Genesis chapters 37-50*)

Paul's Transformation

Before Saul became Paul, he was against those who believed in the Gospel of Jesus Christ. He persecuted everyone who spoke of the Gospel, but on his way to

Damascus, Jesus Himself stopped and blinded him, asking Saul why he was persecuting Him? When he was healed from the blindness through Ananias' prayer, he then had a testimony for himself and proclaimed the same Gospel he persecuted and killed others for. Had Saul not done all the evil he did before his conversion he would not have had the testimony and the Gospel still would not have meant anything to him. After his conversion on the road to Damascus, it is noted in the Bible that his name was changed to Paul. *(Acts 13:9)*

Paul became sold out for Christ from his conversion until his death. Throughout his journey, he was beaten almost to the point of death, he was locked up in prison, in a shipwreck, bitten by a snake etc. He had faith and could endure those things because he had persecuted followers of Christ, and he knew what to expect from the persecutors, but most importantly because his eyes were on the real price (God). His testimony of God healing him from both physical and spiritual blindness was evidence that God had completely delivered him. Being exactly who you were created to be is a great ministry because you will either be glorifying God in your good ways or living for yourself. It is easier to be used by God for His Glory, if you stay true to who He created you to be, just as he did to Paul. Since you were uniquely created, embrace yourself, acknowledge your flaws, own it all, seek to improve yourself, and help those are still struggling, just like Paul did.

> ***Colossians 1:16***
> ***"For in him all things were created: things in heaven and on earth, visible and invisible, whether thrones or powers or rulers or authorities; all things have been created through him and for him."***

Paul went on to write most of the New Testament. God could have used one of the disciples who walked with Jesus, but it may not have been as powerful, because of the disciple's familiarity with Jesus. Paul's conversion was not only for him but also for those who knew who he was, what he did before his transformation, and how God was using him to preach the very Gospel that he had persecuted. Paul used his transformation testimony as the base of his ministry and continued to live his new life in Christ Jesus. Being yourself to the fullest is the best place to begin your balance, because you cannot improve on a character you do not believe is present. Paul's conversion is one of God's balances where we see a complete transformation in a man who turned from his ways and followed the opposite paths of who he used to be (Acts 9:1-19).

BALANCE THROUGH SALVATION

SINCE THE FALL OF MAN (ADAM AND EVE eating the forbidden fruit), sin entered the world and man became sinful by nature. We commonly know that sin is wrong doings, for example lying, cheating, stealing, killing etc. These acts have consequences by law to keep the peace and order in our communities. The laws were first set-in place by God from the Garden of Eden and then later in the ten commandments and several other laws through Moses. When we commit sins, we are rightfully due the consequences, according to what Paul wrote.

Romans 6:23
For the wages of sin is death; but the gift of God
is eternal life through Jesus Christ our Lord.

Christians believe that Salvation is deliverance from sin and its consequences, through faith in Christ Jesus.

Who needs salvation, and how does it bring balance and order?

This is a simple, but complexed question. In order to find out who needs salvation, we ought to also find out how it is received. There is only one way to receive or gain salvation, and it is through Jesus Christ our Lord and Savior. As Christians, we may not be able to live a balanced or the abundant life God promised us, until we receive this gift of salvation.

We all need salvation to be saved from our sins. In the Garden of Eden, the dominion that was given to man by God after creation, was now shifted and man no longer had authority over the earth. The shift caused the devil and his agents to take over what God had given to man and the devil roamed freely on earth because man had sinned against God through disobedience. Our loving Father who created it for us, wanted to give dominion back to man. This time, man had to be bought with the ultimate sacrifice of God's only begotten son, Jesus Christ. He chose a people (the Israelites) specifically from the tribe of Judah, through which His son Jesus was going to be born. Jesus came, lived an exemplary life for us to follow, and died on the cross for us all.

John 3:16
For God so loved the world that he gave his one and only Son, that whoever believes in him shall not perish but have eternal life.

After Jesus' death, all who freely believe, accept Him as the way and the truth, are saved from their sins, gain salvation and are adopted into the Kingdom of God. Before Jesus was crucified on the cross, He taught his disciples how to gain salvation and maintain it. When Thomas was curious about how they can get to the Father, Jesus clarified to him as written in the book of John and the same truth still applies to us today.

John 14:6
Jesus answered, "I am the way and the truth
and the life. No one comes to the Father except
through me.

Paul also provided the steps to salvation in the book
of Romans.

Romans 10:9
If you declare with your mouth, "Jesus is Lord,"
and believe in your heart that God raised him
from the dead, you will be saved.

Notice that the verse begins with "if," which means
it is optional. God has given us the freewill to make the
decision to receive or reject salvation after He sacrificed
His Son for us.

Sometimes when we sacrifice for others, we either
keep reminding them or tell everyone about the help that
was offered. I must admit that there was a time where I
felt used after sacrificing for others, to the point where it
kept me bound. I was expecting that the same good deed
I had done was going to be returned instead of looking to
God for any rewards or blessings. I expected from family
members and friends more than God, but God has a way

of turning things around and making us see Him in every situation we go through, just like the main verse for balance indicates *(Romans 8:28)*. He will allow us to feel let down sometimes, just so we can realize that He is the beginning and end to everything, and He has the ultimate will for our lives. If you feely choose God through Jesus Christ our Savior, He takes full control over your life. God is a Gentleman. He does not force Himself on anyone, though He created us all. He wants us to make the decision, so He gives us the option and freewill. Be sure to make your decision and stand by it.

Why is there a need for freewill when it comes to salvation, if we all need to be saved?

I believe there is a need for us to have freewill because God knows what He has in store for us (our divine purpose), but until we seek Him, we are not sure of the reason for our creation. He sacrificed His only begotten son to show us a glimpse of what He can do for us and how much He loves us. Would you want to give all your treasures to someone, they take it, love it but continuously praise the one who gave nothing up? Our God still blesses us even when we do not know, recognize, thank, or acknowledge Him. Sometimes we go as far as taking what

He has blessed us with to satisfy the schemes of the devil, spending money on things that tear us down, instead of building us up.

> *Isaiah 55:2*
> *Why spend money on what is not bread, and your labor on what does not satisfy? Listen, listen to me, and eat what is good, and you will delight in the richest of fare.*

Before God created us, He knew our end. Make the right choice and begin to experience the life you were created to live and take full advantage of your potentials. Eternal life is the right choice, especially if you want to live a balanced life. Only your Creator can be the balance for you. Most of all, God only wants the pure in heart to see His face.

> *Matthew 5:8*
> *Blessed are the pure in heart, for they will see God.*

Sometimes we are ashamed or afraid of going back to God, but He created us, knows all about us, and knows what we have been through. If you are reading this and you have not accepted Christ in your life and you desire to do so, I would like you to stop here and willingly say this prayer.

> *My heavenly Father, I have sinned against you, I believe in my heart that Your son Jesus Christ came and died on the cross for all my sin., I confess that Jesus is my Lord and Savior who conquered the grave so I can have eternal life. Please come into my life and make me a new person. In Jesus' name I pray. Amen.*

Congratulations on becoming a new being and God will take it from here. The only thing for you to do is increase your desire for Christ and be obedient as the Holy Spirit will lead, guide, and counsel you. You will never be alone, so do not be afraid. Hallelujah!

God wants to give His children nothing less than the best and the only thing we need to do to receive His best is to have a desiring heart. When you have the desire, it is a signal that you are available to be used by God to bless others, the same way you have been blessed. Your gifts are not for you, they are to bless others (that is why they are called gifts), just as you will be blessed through other people's gifts. In order to be used by God, one must be fully balanced. There is a process, and it is usually the ups and downs of life, so embrace it and trust God. When you get the opportunity to be used, you cannot be self-centered, as you may witness what God is doing in others through you, but you do not always get the privilege to see what He is also doing in your own life. Balance is highly needed to achieve a desiring heart, as you will need to know what is already in your heart or what you are lacking. The Holy Spirit will reveal accordingly.

Balance and Order in Wisdom

Wisdom and understanding are important components needed to live a balanced life and these gifts come solely from the Almighty through impartation (sharing). As Christians, we rely on our Bible as a guide to living a Christ like life. When it comes to wisdom, the book of Proverbs is a great guide. It breaks down what wisdom is, and it teaches us how to apply it. Some people are born with wisdom according to their purpose, and some get it (from God) as they travel through life experiences. An example of God generously sharing His wisdom was when King Solomon asked, and he was imparted with the needed wisdom to reign as King of Israel. Given that there is an opposite to everything God creates, the opposite of wisdom is folly (foolishness). Proverbs chapter

9 details the roles of both wisdom and folly. Wisdom extends an invitation to give life to all who accept her, and folly is doing the same, but its invitation is leading to the land of death.

> *Proverbs 9*
> *Wisdom has built her house;*
> *she has set up its seven pillars.*
> *² She has prepared her meat and mixed her wine;*
> *she has also set her table.*
> *³ She has sent out her servants, and she calls*
> *from the highest point of the city,*
> *⁴ "Let all who are simple come to my house!"*
> *To those who have no sense she says,*
> *⁵ "Come, eat my food*
> *and drink the wine I have mixed.*
> *⁶ Leave your simple ways and you will live;*
> *walk in the way of insight."*
> *⁷ Whoever corrects a mocker invites insults;*
> *whoever rebukes the wicked incurs abuse.*
> *⁸ Do not rebuke mockers, or they will hate you;*
> *rebuke the wise and they will love you.*
> *⁹ Instruct the wise and they will be wiser still;*
> *teach the righteous and they will add to*
> *their learning.*

[10] The fear of the Lord is the beginning of wisdom,
and knowledge of the Holy One is understanding.
[11] For through wisdom your days will be many,
and years will be added to your life.
[12] If you are wise, your wisdom will reward you;
if you are a mocker, you alone will suffer.
[13] Folly is an unruly woman;
she is simple and knows nothing.
[14] She sits at the door of her house,
on a seat at the highest point of the city,
[15] calling out to those who pass by,
who go straight on their way,
[16] "Let all who are simple come to my house!"
To those who have no sense she says,
[17] "Stolen water is sweet;
food eaten in secret is delicious!"
[18] But little do they know that the dead are there,
that her guests are deep in the realm of the dead.

Without wisdom, one cannot realize their purpose. The enemy roams around, realizes our purpose, and begins to attack it without us knowing. In my case, there was a time I did not like being emotional as it always comes across as weakness (God created me that way for His purpose). I made efforts to change that personality trait (the enemy attacked it), only because there was no balance in my emotions. I tried to accommodate it by portraying the opposite of the trait (acting emotionless) that only led me to an unhappy place. When the emotions were balanced, God revealed that I need the emotions to be able to empathize with others and discern what they need, but do not need the emotions to get in the way when dealing with spiritual matters. When we do God's work with emotions, it is likely our feelings are going to be hurt just like Jonah's feelings in the book of Jonah *(Chapter 4)*. God sent him to Nineveh, and he did not want to go. He decided to run away from God but in his attempt, God sent a fish to swallow him and he still ended up going to Nineveh. He finally delivered the message to the city, and the king ordered for the Ninevites and their animals to cry out to God for mercy. God heard their cry and had mercy on them. This angered (emotions) Jonah. God proceeded to give him some lessons about how his emotions were not needed in God's merciful decision to the people of Nineveh. One of the fruits of the Spirit is self-control *(Gal. 5:22-23)*. The Holy Spirit can guide and counsel us through wisdom on how to respond to our emotions.

In wisdom, we understand and accept who we are. Being true to yourself is the first step towards a balanced life.

Six steps moving toward living a balanced life

1. *Embrace yourself*

    - Look in your mirror and have an honest conversation with the person in the mirror
    - Talk about what is inside of you (your character)
    - Confront your fears
    - Address your insecurities
    - Acknowledge your difficulties
    - Identify your obstacles
    - Welcome your trials
    - Give yourself the opportunity to feel whatever emotions you are experiencing
    - Unveil your relationships, starting with your relationship with God
    - Recognize every aspect of your life, the good and the bad and own it, because it all makes you.
    - Release the bad and hold on the good parts. Whether you were created with them or you picked them up, in any case let the good parts be the beginning of your scale.

The reason we eat, bath, and look presentable is because we need to maintain our physical appearance, but too often we do not take care of the inside. It is like changing in to clean clothes every day and never bathing. There is a more important need to maintain our mental and inner self than our outer appearances. Remember this consultation begins only between you and your Creator.

2. *Give it to God*

Empty everything you are facing by giving it to God. He promised to help us, and He is waiting with open arms.

Matthew 11:28-29
Come to me, all you who are weary and burdened, and I will give you rest. Take my yoke upon you and learn from me, for I am gentle and humble in heart, and you will find rest for your souls.

3. *Trust the process*

Most things we do, require a process. I love to cook and if you are like me, we can agree that cooking requires a process (recipes) to be effective. To be able to make it through the day, we must follow certain processes like grooming ourselves, and treating our physical, mental and spiritual health right. Sometimes this daily preparation is a struggle, and it will more than likely be the same when you begin your maintenance process after being saved. There will be some challenges as the balancing process takes place. You may lose some relationships because of your transformation but stay focused and stand strong, putting on the whole armor of God.

Ephesians 6:13
Therefore, put on the full armor of God, so that when the day of evil comes, you may be able to stand your ground, and after you have done everything, to stand.

4. *Fill your emptiness*

The feeling of emptiness usually comes when one is not sure of their identity or the reason for their existence. The idea of emptiness is an internal void that can only be permanently filled by the Word of God, which is your weapon (sword), and protecting your mind with the helmet of salvation. When God balances us through His word and salvation, we are made whole.

Ephesians 6:17
Take the helmet of salvation and the sword of the Spirit, which is the word of God.

5. *Personal Revelations*

As you begin to submerge yourself in the Word of God, He starts revealing who you are in the Kingdom through the Holy Spirit. You become alert about all the happenings around you. God starts revealing every perspective concerning you and sheds light on your journey.

- He will put the right people in your path to help you as you travel.
- He will train you to be what He created you to be.
- He will help you with all your struggles.
- He will guide you and order your steps.
- He will comfort you through the Holy Spirit as promised in *John 14:15-18*.
- Ultimately, your purpose will be revealed

6. *Obedience*

Obedience is key when we walk in our purpose because that is how we get guidance and the rewards God saved for us. Being a military spouse, I had to learn how to "Do It Yourself" (DIY) when my husband was deployed to war. One of the things I did was put furniture together and I learned some valuable lessons doing it. Some furniture purchases, require mounting, instructions are usually provided, and the steps need to be strictly followed. The more steps missed, the more likely there will be a malfunction of the item or you could get stuck in the process. In the past, I have turned in pieces to goodwill because I trashed the instructions, got stuck putting them together and could not even go back to the beginning. As you begin to walk in your purpose with God, obedience is vital to all the steps, as it is the only way one can know and follow instructions from God to become balanced. Life does not have a manual, but God knows the end from the beginning, so it is best to get familiar with His voice in your walk.

John 10:27
My sheep listen to my voice; I know them, and
they follow me.

Rewards of a balanced life

When there is a presence of balance in one's life, there are several rewards. Some of the rewards are:

- Order
- Peace
- Gratitude
- Positivity
- Happiness
- Sense of stability
- Freedom
- Abundant life

The most essential reward is to live an abundant life, which is the reason why Jesus came and sacrificed Himself for us. *(Matthew 10:10)*

The consequences of an imbalanced life

There are two major consequences of living an imbalanced life, which are stress and envy.

I. *Stress*

An imbalanced life will create stressful emotions, some of which are, anxiety, fear, shame, anger, and low self-esteem. It can develop from minor things such as not maximizing your day, especially for those of us who are planners. It could just be a late start to the day which leads to falling behind on a schedule, and everything else that follows seems to be a rush, then comes the snowball effect.

Sometimes the enemy preys on things like these and magnifies them to become distractions until we get over-whelmed, then the stress creeps in. Living a balanced life is a continuous checking in with yourself, embracing yourself, and forgiving yourself. When you are balanced, you can easily pinpoint where you are lacking, put more efforts in that area of need, and that keeps you from being overwhelmed. One of the secrets of making your day count is an early rise and being eager to command and take control (allowing the Holy Spirit to guide you) of the day the Lord has blessed you with. When God gave Joshua the instructions to lead the Israelites into the promise land, He did not tell Joshua what time he should start the journey, but he woke up early on the day of, eager to begin the journey *(Joshua 6:12)*

Most people see balance only in the sense of work-life, meanwhile there is a need to find balance in every piece of your life, especially with your inner self. The mind, body and soul are other components that needs to be alignment before that perfect balance can happen. We all should believe in a higher power, for Christians, that higher power is God, who is the head of our lives and in the center of everything we do, providing the needed calm in our existence.

II. *Envy*

When there is envy, it is proof that there is a lack of balance in the person's life. When someone is envious of another person, that means they spend more time looking at that person's life and not concentrating on their own life. They find it difficult to pay attention to their own lives. They are lost in the fascination of someone else's life and forget to count their own blessings. Envy is always accompanied by excuses:

I am not as good-looking.
I was not born with a silver spoon
If only I had that amount of money
I am not blessed with eloquence like them

Good things do not happen to everyone
If I were as tall…
If I were as thin…

The above accusations are some lies from the devil, making us feel less than what we really are. We begin looking at what others possess, and we envy them. The jealousy spirit comes in very subtlety and if you feed it, it will torment you into thinking lies about yourself up to a dangerous point. We ought to fight this spirit with the Word of God.

1 Peter 5:9
Resist him, standing firm in the faith, because you know that the family of believers throughout the world is undergoing the same kind of sufferings.

Most often, Christians suffer with this envious spirit, especially when one of their brother or sisters in Christ seems to be more gifted or anointed than they are, there is usually talks like:

"He/She does not have to catch the Holy Spirit every Sunday."

Why does he/she have to lead songs in the choir every Sunday?

We ought to concentrate on ourselves and accept the purpose God put in us because if He provided the gift, He will provide room for it to be used in the Body of Christ. So, there is no need to be envious of the next person, because a church does not need multiple speakers bringing one word during a service, but the world needs multiple speakers at different times and locations. There is enough vacant room in the Body of Christ.

Matthew 9:37
Then He said to His disciples, "The harvest truly is plentiful, but the laborers are few.

We could be laborers at:
The grocery stores
The club
The bar
On the streets
In our homes
In our neighborhoods
In the desert
In the warzone

The Body of Christ is comprised of many parts and every part of that body is essential. If you are the finger, be the best finger there ever was. There are heavenly rewards awaiting you. Every time you are not doing what you are supposed to be doing (purpose), the Body of Christ is lacking in that part. Wholeness is the goal, but with envy there is lack of completeness, hence no balance and the Body of Christ suffers.

Stress and envy are the top two issues that prevent an individual from finding collective balance. Stress begins with one person, but it affects all who are around, through the different emotions brought on by the stress. Envy is a great personal distraction that involves others and stalls the one who is jealous. These will impact any community's growth and balance.

Balance in Purpose

Our purpose is the reason God created us, which is like a seed He plants inside of the mud. Treasures are normally secured in a chest or kept in a safe. If they are raw materials like diamond in its raw state, they are usually deep in the earth, and you must dig deep into the earth to find a piece. That piece gets refined and then become a treasure to someone. Imagine the refined diamond pieces wrapped in gift boxes and distributed to people. I believe that is how our purposes are securely kept in our bodies by God. We must dig deep and stay connected with God, before the purpose (treasure) is unveiled to us, as it is a process.

2 Corinthians 4:7
But we have this treasure in earthen vessels, that the excellency of the power may be of God, and not of us.

Until there is Balance and Order, our eyes are not opened to the treasure God placed in us. I believe God desires for us to go through the process for training purposes. He uses the challenges that we face as training. The difficulties will make you wiser, build you stronger, create a hedge of protection from the enemy, and make you an expert in your God given purpose. Without this process, you are bound to sabotage it yourself or never even realize what treasure you have inside of you.

As you sojourn through this life, there is a unique journey you are on, which is leading you toward your divine purpose, consciously or unconsciously. For instance, when you are hired for a job, you are trained (in most cases), you grow, and you gradually become an expert at what you do, and you excel. When you shine at your place of employment, it may be easily misunderstood as you have found your purpose, even though for some people it is so. If God had created you with healing as your hidden treasure, and you happen to be in the medical field, you will be exceptional in the profession. You will be graced by God to come up with new inventions and unique cures. You will see people being supernaturally healed, and you will be exposed to all the greatness there is to achieve in that field, as long as you remain obedient. On the other hand, if you are not in the right field, you may be fully educated and knowledgeable in the profession; however, you will always feel a void or unfulfilled/unhappy. Many people are in the wrong places because of convenience, money, or just being disconnected. The earlier you plug in with God for your purpose to be revealed, the better things will be for you in your lifetime. It is expected to make mistakes when we are young, so we can benefit from that notion because we are more forgiving of our younger selves than our older selves. Only God can restore, and He is able to do it the moment we submit to Him and His will for our lives no matter our age. Sarah's purpose was fulfilled at age 90, when she gave birth to Isaac, even though she had given up and it was no longer deemed possible scientifically. God kept to the promise that He gave Abraham, that he will bear a child with Sarah and become the father of many Nations. To be in a perfect balance and order, it is necessary to be in your purpose (the reason for your existence) because in our purpose, there is peace, joy, happiness, prosperity, success, abundant life and all your heart desires. It is never too late or too early to live a purposeful, abundant, happy, balanced, and orderly life. Get connected with God and let Him reinstate order in your life.

God's Order is not man's Order

As we embark on our journey in the quest for a balanced and orderly life, sometimes God's order will not look like the right order, but it is vital to trust Him. Most of the time our purposes are so grand that if God were to reveal it all at once to us, it may consume us. When Lucifer discovered how God had separated him from the rest of the angels, he became proud and even attempted to be like God and share of God's glory. His pride caused him to be thrown out of heaven forever. Stay your course, and do not put too much emphasis on the mysteries of God, how He is ordering your steps, because you may get caught up into the mysteries and miss what He is doing in the season. Only God knows how He is ordering our steps.

2 Corinthians 4:18
So, we fix our eyes not on what is seen, but on what is unseen, since what is seen is temporary, but what is unseen is eternal.

Here are a couple of examples of God's order that defies man's intellect:

1. Mary's conception of Jesus was not the order we know, and could have caused Joseph not to marry Mary, but there was peace in the marriage because it was God's order.

2. When Samuel went to anoint the new King of Israel in the house of Jesse, David was not invited by his own father to see if he made the cut. According to Jesse (David's father), David did not fit the description of a King. Once again, God's order was not the usual.

Isaiah 55:8
For my thoughts are not your thoughts, neither are your ways my ways, saith the **Lord.**

How to maintain Balance

It may be easy to acquire a balance but how can one maintain and sustain it? When we purchase a vehicle, we need to keep up with the maintenance, washing the car every so often, using the right fuel type, and taking it to the body shop for overall maintenance. If we do not keep it up, the car will eventually stop running. In the same manner we need to maintain our physical, mental, and spiritual aspects for our balance to align.

- The physical part is maintained by eating right, exercising, regular Doctors visits to maintain our bodies.
- Mental maintenance requires your emotional well-being (be sure to seek counseling if you need it).
- The spiritual maintenance is your relationship with God, and it is the most important because when we are connected, we get the wisdom to maintain all components.

When things in our personal life changes, there is a need for a new balance. In my case as mentioned earlier, the first time I felt a tremendous difference in my balance was when I lost my mother. I felt like everything on one side of my scale was completely emptied and I had a feeling of being lopsided for a couple of years. Shortly after that, I moved to Germany and felt like somethings were being put back on the other side of the scale for a better balance. I felt hopeful again and from that hope, God started adding peace, joy, and happiness. Meeting my husband was a great addition to the other side of my scale. Due to our friendships, we could laugh about silly things for hours and that laughter gradually soothed my pain subconsciously. I know now that God was putting a path before me. He is our Creator and knows exactly how we can maintain the balance in every aspect, level, and step of the journey.

Ministry Maintenance

Whatever your purpose is, it becomes your ministry. Anyone who is already functioning in their ministry can attest to the fact that there is a great need to find balance. If not, a piece of your life will suffer the consequences of the imbalance. If you are married with children, that should be your first ministry. God takes pride in a family unit, so as a married couple or parent, you will have to maintain your spouse and children, making sure all is well in the home. If not, there will be a need for balance in those areas. If possible, it is important to frequently seek maintenance of your family and friends' relationships as well, because you need a support system. The entire book of John is a great manual of love and different relationships.

This balance is important because sometimes in your walk, you need to spend time alone with God for Him to download His mysteries in relation to His will for your life. If there is no balance in your personal life and your relationships, your ministry will suffer and that is not what God intends for you to go through. Moses had to spend 40 years in Midian as a shepherd after running away from Egypt. He thought he was running away because he secretly murdered an Egyptian in rebellion, and the secret was out. Little did he know that God was isolating him to prepare him to go back to Egypt and lead the Israelites out of slavery. I usually refer to the isolation period as "season in wilderness." Sometimes our wilderness experience may seem strange to our friends, family, and many people but we must get the complete reason of the isolation before we can move to the next level. During this time, things and people come off our scales, some may or may not be put back. Some of the people and things we hold on to are not part of what God is doing in the season.

I was never a heavy drinker, but I drank alcohol socially, during my isolation process, God took the appetite away and I did not even realize until six months later. I tried drinking a glass of wine and it tasted bitter in my mouth. Since then, almost four years now, I have not had a sip of alcohol and do not miss it. He allowed me to notice that change, but I am certain that there are several other things He delivered me from that I may never even know.

Hebrews 12:1
Therefore, we also, since we are surrounded by so great a cloud of witnesses, let us lay aside every weight, and the sin which so easily ensnares us, and let us run with endurance the race that is set before us,

Family Maintenance

This can be challenging at times to go through the process of balance because of the love we have for our families, but we often forget that God loved us individually first, before placing us as a family unit. Family units from creation has been dear to God, especially because of the fellowship piece. The best family maintenance when you are on your journey of finding your order and balance, is to be patient with your loved ones because most often they do not understand what is going on with you. Trust God with your family, He will maintain everybody while you journey with Him and there will be understanding.

CONCLUSION

IT IS MY PRAYER THAT BY THIS POINT IN the book, you have been able to see how God helped to put balance and order in my life and you are able to identify some things that He can help you with to get to your purpose of existence. Whatever level, stage, or season you are in your life, if you still have breath and are reading this book, I want to assure you that there is hope. God loves you so much that He is willing to leave ninety-nine of His children and come looking for you. You are important to Him and He wants to spend eternity with you, in the mansion He has prepared for you. God is a Father like none other, His grace and mercy are endless, He sacrificed His only son so you can live a free and abundant life. Put God at the center of your life, try Him, trust Him, and taste and see how good God is. He will bring balance and order into your life that you have never experienced. You have nothing to lose but you have everything (eternal life) to gain!

Father in heaven, I thank you for the grace to write this book and for my brother/sister reading it. I know it is not a coincidence because everything You do is intentional. You alone know what they stand in need of and I pray that You not only grant their desires, but please Father, manifest Yourself in their lives. May they receive what they need to continue Your work here on earth and when it is all set and done, You will welcome us by saying "Well done, good and faithful servant!" In Jesus' name I pray. Amen

CPSIA information can be obtained
at www.ICGtesting.com
Printed in the USA
BVHW042225130421
604819BV00009BA/1326